The Ultimate

COSORI

Air Fryer Cookbook

Delicious and Healthy Air Fryer Recipes to Enjoy the
Crispness of Your Cosori Air Fryer

Air Fryer Lab

Table of Content

Breakfast

1. Mushroom Frittata

Preparation Time: 10 minutes

Cooking Time: 13 minutes

Servings: 1

Ingredients:

- 1 cup egg whites
- 1 cup spinach, chopped
- 2 mushrooms, sliced
- 2 tbsp. parmesan cheese, grated
- Salt

Directions:

1. Sprinkle pan with cooking spray and heat over medium heat. Add mushrooms and sauté for 2-3 minutes Add spinach and cook for 1-2 minutes or until wilted.

2. Transfer mushroom spinach mixture into the air fryer pan. Beat egg whites in a mixing bowl until frothy. Season it with a pinch of salt.

3. Pour egg white mixture into the spinach and mushroom mixture and sprinkle with parmesan cheese. Place pan in air fryer basket and cook frittata at 350 F for 8 minutes

4. Slice and serve.

Nutrition: Calories 176 Fat 3 g Carbs 4 g Protein 31 g

2. Egg Muffins

Preparation Time: 10 minutes

Cooking Time: 15 minutes

Servings: 12

Ingredients:

- 9 eggs
- 1/2 cup onion, sliced
- 1 tbsp. olive oil
- 8 oz. ground sausage
- 1/4 cup coconut milk
- 1/2 tsp oregano
- 1 1/2 cups spinach
- 3/4 cup bell peppers, chopped
- Pepper
- Salt

Directions:

1. Preheat the air fryer to 325 F.
2. Add ground sausage in a pan and sauté over medium heat for 5 minutes
3. Add olive oil, oregano, bell pepper, and onion and sauté until onion is translucent.
4. Put spinach to the pan and cook for 30 seconds.
5. Remove pan from heat and set aside.

6. In a mixing bowl, whisk together eggs, coconut milk, pepper, and salt until well beaten.

7. Add sausage and vegetable mixture into the egg mixture and mix well.

8. Pour egg mixture into the silicone muffin molds and place into the air fryer basket. (Cook in batches)

9. Cook muffins for 15 minutes

10. Serve and enjoy.

Nutrition: Calories 135 Fat 11 g Carbs 1.5 g Protein 8 g

3. Blueberry Breakfast Cobbler

Preparation Time: 5 minutes

Cooking Time: 15 minutes

Servings: 4

Ingredients:

- ⅓ cup whole-wheat pastry flour
- ¾ teaspoon baking powder
- Dash sea salt
- ½ cup 2% milk
- 2 tablespoons pure maple syrup
- ½ teaspoon vanilla extract
- Cooking oil spray
- ½ cup fresh blueberries
- ¼ cup Granola, or plain store-bought granola

Directions:

1. In a medium bowl, whisk the flour, baking powder, and salt. Add the milk, maple syrup, and vanilla and gently whisk, just until thoroughly combined.

2. Preheat the unit by selecting BAKE, setting the temperature to 350°F, and setting the time to 3 minutes Select START/STOP to start.

3. Spray a 6-by-2-inch round baking pan with cooking oil and pour the batter into the pan. Top evenly with the blueberries and granola.

4. Once the unit is preheated, place the pan into the basket.

5. Select BAKE, set the temperature to 350°F, and set the time to 15 minutes Select START/STOP to begin.

6. When the cooking is complete, the cobbler should be nicely browned and a knife inserted into the middle should come out clean. Enjoy plain or topped with a little vanilla yogurt.

Nutrition: Calories 112 Fat 1g Carbs 23g Protein 3g

4. Granola

Preparation Time: 5 minutes

Cooking Time: 40 minutes

Servings: 2

Ingredients:

- 1 cup rolled oats
- 3 tablespoons pure maple syrup
- 1 tablespoon sugar
- 1 tablespoon neutral-flavored oil, such as refined coconut, sunflower, or safflower
- ¼ teaspoon sea salt
- ¼ teaspoon ground cinnamon
- ¼ teaspoon vanilla extract

Directions:

1. Insert the crisper plate into the basket and the basket into the unit. Preheat the unit by selecting BAKE, setting the temperature to 250°F, and setting the time to 3 minutes Select START/STOP to start.

2. In a medium bowl, stir together the oats, maple syrup, sugar, oil, salt, cinnamon, and vanilla until thoroughly combined. Transfer the granola to a 6-by-2-inch round baking pan.

3. Once the unit is preheated, place the pan into the basket.

4. Select BAKE, set the temperature to 250°F and set the time to 40 minutes Select START/STOP to begin. After 10 minutes, stir the granola well. Resume cooking, stirring the granola every 10 minutes, for a total of 40 minutes, or until the granola is lightly browned and mostly dry.

5. Place the granola on a plate to cool, when the cooking is complete. It will become crisp as it cools. Store the completely cooled granola in an airtight container in a cool, dry place for 1 to 2 weeks.

6. Variation Tip: You can change this recipe to include some of your favorite granola ingredients, such as dried fruits, different types of nuts, and even goodies such as chocolate chips. Stir them in after the granola is done, but before it's completely cool.

Nutrition: Calories 165 Fat 5g Carbs 27g Protein 3g

5. Mixed Berry Muffins

Preparation Time: 15 minutes

Cooking Time: 15 minutes

Servings: 8

Ingredients:

- 1⅓ cups plus 1 tablespoon all-purpose flour, divided
- ¼ cup granulated sugar
- 2 tablespoons light brown sugar
- 2 teaspoons baking powder
- 2 eggs
- ⅔Cup whole milk
- ⅓Cup safflower oil
- 1 cup mixed fresh berries

Directions:

1. In a medium bowl, stir together 1⅓ cups of flour, the granulated sugar, brown sugar, and baking powder until mixed well.

2. In a small bowl, whisk the eggs, milk, and oil until combined. Mix the egg mixture into the dry ingredients just until combined.

3. In another small bowl, toss the mixed berries with the left over 1 tablespoon of flour until coated. Gently stir the berries into the batter.

4. Two times the 16 foil muffin cups to make 8 cups.

5. Insert the crisper plate into the basket and the basket into the unit. Preheat the unit by selecting BAKE, setting the temperature to 315°F, and setting the time to 3 minutes Select START/STOP to start.

6. Once the unit is preheated, place 4 cups into the basket and fill each three-quarter full with the batter.

7. Select BAKE, set the temperature to 315°F, and set the time for 17 minutes Select START/STOP to begin.

8. After about 12 minutes, check the muffins. If they spring back when lightly touched with your finger, they are done. If not, resume cooking. When the cooking is done, transfer the muffins to a wire rack to cool. Repeat steps 6, 7, and 8 with the remaining muffin cups and batter. Let the muffins cool for 10 minutes before serving.

Nutrition: Calories 230 Fat 11g Carbs 30g Protein 4g

6. Homemade Strawberry Breakfast Tarts

Preparation Time: 15 minutes

Cooking Time: 20 minutes

Servings: 6

Ingredients:

- 2 refrigerated piecrusts
- ½ cup strawberry preserves
- 1 teaspoon cornstarch
- Cooking oil spray
- ½ cup low-fat vanilla yogurt
- 1-ounce cream cheese, at room temperature
- 3 tablespoons confectioners' sugar
- Rainbow sprinkles, for decorating

Directions:

1. Place the piecrusts on a flat surface. Cut each piecrust into 3 rectangles using a knife or pizza cutter, for 6 in total. Discard any unused dough from the piecrust edges.

2. In a small bowl, stir together the preserves and cornstarch. Mix well, ensuring there are no lumps of cornstarch remaining.

3. Scoop 1 tablespoon of the strawberry mixture onto the top half of each piece of piecrust.

4. Fold the bottom of each piece up to enclose the filling. Press along the edges of each tart to seal using the back of a fork.

5. Insert the crisper plate into the basket and the basket into the unit. Preheat the unit by selecting bake, setting the temperature to 375°F, and setting the time to 3 minutes Select start/stop to start.

6. Once the unit is preheated, spray the crisper plate with cooking oil. Work in batches, spray the breakfast tarts with cooking oil and place them into the basket in a single layer. Do not stack the tarts.

7. Select bake, set the temperature to 375°F, and set the time to 10 minutes Select start/stop to begin.

8. When the cooking is complete, the tarts should be light golden brown. Let the breakfast tarts cool fully before removing them from the basket.

9. Repeat steps 5, 6, 7, and 8 for the remaining breakfast tarts.

10. In a small bowl, stir together the yogurt, cream cheese, and confectioners' sugar. Spread the breakfast tarts with the frosting and top with sprinkles.

Nutrition: Calories 408 Fat 20.5g Carbs 56g Protein 1g

7. Everything Bagels

Preparation Time: 10 minutes

Cooking Time: 10 minutes

Servings: 2

Ingredients:

- ½ cup self-rising flour, plus more for dusting
- ½ cup plain Greek yogurt
- 1 egg
- 1 tablespoon water
- 4 teaspoons everything bagel spice mix
- Cooking oil spray
- 1 tablespoon butter, melted

Directions:

1. In a large bowl, using a wooden spoon, stir together the flour and yogurt until a tacky dough forms. Transfer the dough to a lightly floured work surface and roll the dough into a ball.

2. Cut the dough into 2 pieces and roll each piece into a log. Form each log into a bagel shape, pinching the ends together.

3. In a small bowl, whisk the egg and water. Brush the egg wash on the bagels.

4. Sprinkle 2 teaspoons of the spice mix on each bagel and gently press it into the dough.

5. Insert the crisper plate into the basket and the basket into the unit. Preheat the unit by selecting bake, setting the temperature to 330°F, and setting the time to 3 minutes Select start/stop to begin.

6. Once the unit is preheated, spray the crisper plate with cooking spray. Drizzle with the bagels with the butter and place them into the basket.

7. Select BAKE, set the temperature to 330°F, and set the time to 10 minutes Select START/STOP to begin.

8. When the cooking is complete, the bagels should be lightly golden on the outside. Serve warm.

Nutrition: Calories 271 Fat 13g Carbs 28g Protein 10g

Main Dishes

8. Pork Belly in Wine

Preparation Time: 10 minutes

Cooking Time: 50 minutes

Servings: 3

Ingredients:

- 20 oz pork belly

- 1 cup of onions, peeled and chopped

- 1 cup of white wine

- 3 tablespoons avocado oil

- 4 garlic cloves, minced

- ¼ teaspoon red pepper flakes

- 3 teaspoons sesame seeds

Directions:

1. In a bowl, combine the belly, pepper, onions, tomato sauce, garlic, oil, pepper flakes and sesame seeds and toss well. Pour the wine and marinate the pork for a couple of hours at room temperature or place in the fridge overnight. Add it to your air fryer and close the lid to cook on a HIGH pressure for around 40 minutes.

2. Open the lid and place the pork on the cutting board and slice it.

3. Return the pork to the air fryer and Put the air fryer to sauté mode.

4. Cook the pork for 10 minutes and portion it into three plates and dollop each plate with some sesame seeds.

Nutrition: Calories 223 Protein 42 g. Fat 48 g. Carbs 189 g.

9. Pork Meat and Pumpkin

Preparation Time: 10 minutes

Cooking Time: 55 minutes

Servings: 3

Ingredients:

- 2 pieces of ½ inch thick bone-in pork loin or rib
- 1 medium pumpkin, peeled and diced
- 4 tablespoons dried sage
- 2 tablespoons clarified and unsalted butter
- 2 teaspoons dried thyme
- 2 teaspoons ground cinnamon
- 1 cup of chicken broth
- 1 teaspoon of salt
- 1 teaspoon pepper

Directions:

1. Fix your Air fryer to sauté mode and melt the unsalted butter or use the skillet to melt the butter and then pour it into your Air fryer.

2. Combine the salt, pepper, dried thyme, sage and cinnamonIn a bowl,. Season the pork meat with the spices mix and toss it in the unsalted butter to cook for 10 minutes.

3. Then, add in the pumpkin and pour in the chicken broth.

4. Make sure to lock the lid and cook on high pressure for 45 minutes.

5. Quick-release the pressure and transfer the pork to a plate.

6. Spoon the pumpkin around the pork nicely and ladle up the sauce (if any) all over the meat. Serve it with the cold beer.

Nutrition: Calories 386 Protein 77 g. Fat 81 g. Carbs 286 g.

10.   Spicy Instant Pork with Peanuts

Preparation Time: 15 minutes

Cooking Time: 55 minutes

Servings: 4

Ingredients:

- 25 oz pork, ground
- ½ large onion, chopped
- 1 cup of peanuts
- 1 garlic clove, minced
- 1 bay leaf
- 2 ounces tomato sauce
- 1 tablespoon olives, pitted
- 1 tablespoon cilantro, chopped
- ½ cup of water
- 2 teaspoon chili powder
- Salt and pepper, to taste

Directions:

1. Preheat the oven to 240°-260°F and roast the peanuts in the oven for 10 minutes until crispy and then let it cool completely. Then grind the peanuts using a food processor or blender.

2. Marinate the pork in the salt, pepper and chili powder for a couple of hours at room temperature or place in the fridge overnight. Fix the Air fryer to sauté mode and add in the pork. Break the pork meat into pieces and cook until browned.

3. Add in remaining ingredients and mix well.

4. Make sure to lock the lid and cook on HIGH pressure for 45 minutes.

5. Then portion the pork into four plates. Serve it with the salad and brown rice.

Nutrition: Calories 381 Protein 71 g. Fat 78 g. Carbs 282 g.

Preparation Time: 20 minutes

Cooking Time: 1 hour and 20 minutes

Servings: 6-8

Ingredients:

- 2 tablespoons canola oil

- 1 (3-pound) beef chuck roast

- Kosher salt

- Freshly ground black pepper

- 1 large onion, halved and sliced

- 4 garlic cloves, minced

- 4 fresh thyme sprigs

- 1 bay leaf

- 1¾ cups or 1 (14.5-ounce) can beef broth

- 1 pound new potatoes, halved, no bigger than 1-inch pieces

- 4 to 5 large carrots, cut into ¾-inch pieces

- 3 large parsnips, cut into ¾-inch pieces

Directions:

1. To preheat the Air fryer, Choose Sauté on high heat. Add the oil.

2. Season the roast with salt and pepper. Once the pot is hot, brown the roast on all sides, 3 to 4 minutes per side. Transfer the meat to a plate.

3. Add the onion and cook for 3 to 5 minutes until starting to brown. Add the garlic, thyme, bay leaf, and broth. Scrape the bottom of the pot to deglaze the pan. Return the meat to the pot and secure the lid.

4. Select Manual or Pressure Cook and cook at high pressure for 1 hour.

5. Once cooking is done, use a quick release. Add the potatoes, carrots, and parsnips, submerging them in the cooking liquid.

6. Select Manual or Pressure Cook and cook at high heat for 10 minutes.

7. When cooking is complete, use a natural release for 10 minutes and then release any remaining steam.

8. The potatoes should be fork-tender and the meat should be falling apart. Serve topped with the juice.

Nutrition: Calories 1011 Protein 64 g. Fat 26 g. Carbs 32 g.

12.   One-Pot Pasta Bolognese

Preparation Time: 10 minutes

Cooking Time: 5 minutes

Servings: 4

Ingredients:

- 1 tablespoon extra-virgin olive oil

- 12 ounces lean ground beef

- 1 large onion, chopped

- 3 garlic cloves, minced

- ½ cup dry red wine

- ½ teaspoon kosher salt, plus more for seasoning

- ¼ teaspoon red pepper flakes

- 1½ cups water

- 12 ounces uncooked penne pasta (with a 9to 13-minute cook time)

- 1 (28-ounce) can crushed tomatoes in purée or good tomato sauce

- ½ cup shredded mozzarella cheese

Directions

1. Heat up the Air fryer by choosing Sauté on high heat.

2. Wait 1 minute and then add the oil. Add the ground beef and use a wooden spoon or spatula to break up and stir as it cooks, about 3 minutes.

3. Once the meat is cooked, putin the onion and stir. Cook for 1 minute and add the garlic. Cook for 1 minute more.

4. Add the wine and rake off the bottom to deglaze the pan. Cook for 1 to 2 minutes, or once the alcohol smell has gone away.

5. Add the salt, red pepper flakes, and water and stir. Add the pasta and stir. Pour the tomatoes or tomato sauce over in an even layer, covering the pasta. Secure the lid.

6. Select Manual or Pressure Cook and cook at high pressure for 5 minutes

7. As soon as done cooking, use a quick release. Test the pasta. If it isn't quite done, Choose Sauté and simmer for another 1 to 2 minutes. Serve topped with mozzarella.

Nutrition: Calories 596 Protein 45 g. Fat 4 g. Carbs 68 g.

13. Five-Spice Boneless Beef Ribs

Preparation Time: 15 minutes

Cooking Time: 35 minutes

Servings: 6

Ingredients:

- 6 boneless beef short ribs, trimmed

- 2 teaspoons Chinese five-spice powder

- Kosher salt

- 2 tablespoons canola oil

- 4 garlic cloves, minced

- 1-inch piece fresh ginger, finely chopped

- 2 tablespoons rice wine vinegar

- ½ cup beef broth

- ¼ cup soy sauce

- ¼ cup raw sugar or brown sugar

Directions:

1. Preheat the oven to broil.

2. Coat the ribs with the five-spice powder and season with salt. Place on a baking sheet and broil them for 3 minutes on each side.

3. Preheat the Air fryer by selecting Sauté. Add the oil

4. Put the garlic and ginger and sauté for 2 minutes, until starting to brown. Add in the vinegar and cook for another minute. Select Cancel and add the broth, soy sauce, and sugar and stir until the sugar dissolves. Add the ribs and secure the lid.

5. Select Manual or Pressure Cook and cook at high pressure for 35 minutes

6. Once done cooking, use a natural release. This will take about 15 minutes.

7. Take out the ribs and put them back on the baking sheet. Brush with the cooking liquid and broil again for 3 minutes per side to form a crust.

8. Meanwhile, Choose Sauté on high heat and reduce the sauce by up to half.

9. After broiling, brush the ribs on all sides with the sauce. Serve with extra sauce.

Nutrition: Calories 247 Protein 27 g. Fat 2 g. Carbs 10 g.

14.   Cauliflower, Okra, and Pepper Casserole

Preparation Time: 8 minutes

Cooking Time: 12 minutes

Servings: 4

Ingredients:

- 1 head cauliflower, cut into florets
- 1 cup okra, chopped
- 1 yellow bell pepper, chopped
- 2 eggs, beaten
- 1/2 cup chopped onion
- 1 tablespoon soy sauce
- 2 tablespoons olive oil
- Salt and ground black pepper, to taste

Directions:

1. Spritz a baking pan with cooking spray.

2. Put the cauliflower in a food processor and pulse to rice the cauliflower.

3. Pour the cauliflower rice in the baking pan and add the remaining ingredients. Stir to mix well.

4. Place the pan on the bake position.

5. Select Bake, set temperature to 380°F (193°C) and set time to 12 minutes.

6. When cooking is complete, the eggs should be set.

7.   Remove the baking pan from the air fryer grill and serve immediately.

Nutrition: Calories 246 Carbs 0.1g Fat 2.8g Protein 10.8g

Preparation Time: 15 minutes

Cooking Time: 12 minutes

Servings: 4

Ingredients:

- 1 cup cooked chicken, shredded
- ¼ cup Greek yogurt
- ¼ cup salsa
- 1 cup shredded Mozzarella cheese
- Salt and ground black pepper, to taste
- 4 flour tortillas
- Cooking spray

Directions:

1. Spritz the air fry basket with cooking spray.

2. Combine all the ingredients, except for the tortillas, in a large bowl. Stir to mix well.

3. Make the taquitos: Unfold the tortillas on a clean work surface, then scoop up 2 tablespoons of the chicken mixture in the middle of each tortilla. Roll the tortillas up to wrap the filling.

4. Arrange the taquitos in the basket and spritz with cooking spray.

5. Place the basket on the air fry position.

6. Select Air Fry, set temperature to 380°F (193°C) and set time to 12 minutes. Flip the taquitos halfway through the cooking time.

7. When cooked, the taquitos should be golden brown and the cheese should be melted.

8. Serve immediately.

Nutrition: Calories 256 Carbs 0.1g Fat 2.8g Protein 10.8g

Meat & Poultry

16.   Easy Ritzy Chicken Nuggets

Preparation Time: 20 minutes

Cooking Time: 8 minutes

Servings: 4

Ingredients:

- 1 ½ pounds chicken tenderloins, cut into small pieces
- 1/2 teaspoon garlic salt
- 1/2 teaspoon cayenne pepper
- 1/4 teaspoon black pepper, freshly cracked
- 4 tablespoons olive oil
- 1/3 cup saltines (e.g. Ritz crackers), crushed
- 4 tablespoons Parmesan cheese, freshly grated

Directions:

1. Start by preheating your Air Fryer to 390 degrees F.

2. Season each piece of the chicken with garlic salt, cayenne pepper, and black pepper.

3. In a mixing bowl, thoroughly combine the olive oil with crushed saltines. Dip each piece of chicken in the cracker mixture.

4. Finally, roll the chicken pieces over the Parmesan cheese. Cook for 8 minutes, working in batches.

5. Later, if you want to warm the chicken nuggets, add them to the basket and cook for 1 minute more. Serve with French fries, if desired.

Nutrition: 355 Calories 20.1g Fat 5.3g Carbs 36.6g Protein 0.2g Sugars

17.   Asian Chicken Filets with Cheese

Preparation Time: 50 minutes

Cooking Time: 20 minutes

Servings: 2

Ingredients:

- 4 rashers smoked bacon
- 2 chicken filets
- 1/2 teaspoon coarse sea salt
- 1/4 teaspoon black pepper, preferably freshly ground
- 1 teaspoon garlic, minced
- 1 (2-inch) piece ginger, peeled and minced
- 1 teaspoon black mustard seeds
- 1 teaspoon mild curry powder
- 1/2 cup coconut milk
- 1/3 cup tortilla chips, crushed
- 1/2 cup Pecorino Romano cheese, freshly grated

Directions:

1. Start by preheating your Air Fryer to 400 degrees F. Add the smoked bacon and cook in the preheated Air Fryer for 5 to 7 minutes. Reserve.

2. In a mixing bowl, place the chicken fillets, salt, black pepper, garlic, ginger, mustard seeds, curry powder, and milk. Let it marinate in your refrigerator about 30 minutes.

3. In another bowl, mix the crushed chips and grated Pecorino Romano cheese.

4. Dredge the chicken fillets through the chips mixture and transfer them to the cooking basket. Reduce the temperature to 380 degrees F and cook the chicken for 6 minutes.

5. Turn them over and cook for a further 6 minutes. Repeat the process until you have run out of ingredients.

6. Serve with reserved bacon. Enjoy!

Nutrition: 376 Calories 19.6g Fat 12.1g Carbs 36.2g Protein 3.4g Sugars

18. Paprika Chicken Legs With Brussels Sprouts

Preparation Time: 30 minutes

Cooking Time: 20 minutes

Servings: 2

Ingredients:

- 2 chicken legs

- 1/2 teaspoon paprika

- 1/2 teaspoon kosher salt

- 1/2 teaspoon black pepper

- 1-pound Brussels sprouts

- 1 teaspoon dill, fresh or dried

Directions:

1. Start by preheating your Air Fryer to 370 degrees F.

2. Now, season your chicken with paprika, salt, and pepper. Transfer the chicken legs to the cooking basket. Cook for 10 minutes.

3. Flip the chicken legs and cook an additional 10 minutes. Reserve.

4. Add the Brussels sprouts to the cooking basket; sprinkle with dill. Cook at 380 degrees F for 15 minutes, shaking the basket halfway through.

5. Serve with the reserved chicken legs. Bon appétit!

Nutrition: 355 Calories 20.1g Fat 5.3g Carbs 36.6g Protein 0.2g Sugars

19.   Chinese Duck

Preparation Time: 30 minutes

Cooking Time: 20 minutes

Servings: 6

Ingredients:

- 2 pounds duck breast, boneless
- 2 green onions, chopped
- 1 tablespoon light soy sauce
- 1 teaspoon Chinese 5-spice powder
- 1 teaspoon Szechuan peppercorns
- 3 tablespoons Shaoxing rice wine
- 1 teaspoon coarse salt
- 1/2 teaspoon ground black pepper

Glaze:

- 1/4 cup molasses
- 3 tablespoons orange juice
- 1 tablespoon soy sauce

Directions:

1. In a ceramic bowl, place the duck breasts, green onions, light soy sauce, Chinese 5-spice powder, Szechuan peppercorns, and Shaoxing rice wine. Let it marinate for 1 hour in your refrigerator.

2. Preheat your Air Fryer to 400 degrees F for 5 minutes.

3. Now, discard the marinade and season the duck breasts with salt and pepper. Cook the duck breasts for 12 to 15 minutes or until they are golden brown. Repeat with the other ingredients.

4. In the meantime, add the reserved marinade to the saucepan that is preheated over medium-high heat. Add the molasses, orange juice, and 1 tablespoon of soy sauce.

5. Bring to a simmer and then, whisk constantly until it gets syrupy. Brush the surface of duck breasts with glaze so they are completely covered.

6. Place duck breasts back in the Air Fryer basket; cook an additional 5 minutes. Enjoy!

Nutrition: 403 Calories 25.3g Fat 16.4g Carbs 27.5g Protein 13.2g Sugars

20.   Turkey Bacon with Scrambled Eggs

Preparation Time: 25 minutes

Cooking Time: 20 minutes

Servings: 4

Ingredients:

- 1/2-pound turkey bacon

- 4 eggs

- 1/3 cup milk

- 2 tablespoons yogurt

- 1/2 teaspoon sea salt

- 1 bell pepper, finely chopped

- 2 green onions, finely chopped

- 1/2 cup Colby cheese, shredded

Directions:

1. Place the turkey bacon in the cooking basket.

2. Cook at 360 degrees F for 9 to 11 minutes. Work in batches. Reserve the fried bacon.

3. In a mixing bowl, thoroughly whisk the eggs with milk and yogurt. Add salt, bell pepper, and green onions.

4. Brush the sides and bottom of the baking pan with the reserved 1 teaspoon of bacon grease.

5. Pour the egg mixture into the baking pan. Cook at 355 degrees F about 5 minutes. Top with shredded Colby cheese and cook for 5 to 6 minutes more.

6. Serve the scrambled eggs with the reserved bacon and enjoy!

Nutrition: 456 Calories 38.3g Fat 6.3g Carbs1.4g Protein 4.5g Sugars

Preparation Time: 25 minutes ago

Cooking Time: 20 minutes

Servings: 4

Ingredients:

- 1 (1-pound) fillet chicken breast

- Sea salt and ground black pepper, to taste

- 1 tablespoon olive oil

- 4 eggs

- 1/2 teaspoon cayenne pepper

- 1/2 cup Mascarpone cream

- 1/4 cup Asiago cheese, freshly grated

Directions:

1. Flatten the chicken breast with a meat mallet. Season with salt and pepper.

2. Heat the olive oil in a frying pan over medium flame. Cook the chicken for 10 to 12 minutes; slice into small strips, and reserve.

3. Then, in a mixing bowl, thoroughly combine the eggs, and cayenne pepper; season with salt to taste. Add the cheese and stir to combine.

4. Add the reserved chicken. Then, pour the mixture into a lightly greased pan; put the pan into the cooking basket.

5. Cook in the preheated Air Fryer at 355 degrees F for 10 minutes, flipping over halfway through.

Nutrition: 329 Calories 25.3g Fat 3.4g Carbs 21.1g Protei2.3g Sugars

22.   Flavorful Steak

Preparation Time: 10 minutes

Cooking Time: 18 minutes

Servings: 2

Ingredients:

- 2 steaks, rinsed and pat dry
- ½ tsp garlic powder
- 1 tsp olive oil
- Pepper
- Salt

Directions:

1. Rub steaks with olive oil and season with garlic powder, pepper, and salt.

2. Preheat the air fryer oven to 400 F.

3. Place steaks on air fryer oven pan and air fry for 10-18 minutes turn halfway through.

4. Serve and enjoy.

Nutrition: Calories 361 Fat 10.9 g Carbs 0.5 g Protein 61.6 g

23. Lemon Garlic Lamb Chops

Preparation Time: 10 minutes

Cooking Time: 6 minutes

Servings: 6

Ingredients:

- 6 lamb loin chops
- 2 tbsp. fresh lemon juice
- 1 ½ tbsp. lemon zest
- 1 tbsp. dried rosemary
- 1 tbsp. olive oil
- 1 tbsp. garlic, minced
- Pepper
- Salt

Directions:

1. Add lamb chops in a mixing bowl. Add remaining ingredients on top of lamb chops and coat well.

2. Arrange lamb chops on air fryer oven tray and air fry at 400 F for 3 minutes. Turn lamb chops to another side and air fry for 3 minutes more. Serve and enjoy.

Nutrition: Calories 69 Fat 6 g Carbs 1.2 g Protein 3 g

24. Herb Butter Rib-eye Steak

Preparation Time: 10 minutes

Cooking Time: 14 minutes

Servings: 4

Ingredients:

- 2 lbs. rib eye steak, bone-in
- 1 tsp fresh rosemary, chopped
- 1 tsp fresh thyme, chopped
- 1 tsp fresh chives, chopped
- 2 tsp fresh parsley, chopped
- 1 tsp garlic, minced
- ¼ cup butter softened
- Pepper
- Salt

Directions:

1. In a small bowl, combine together butter and herbs.
2. Rub herb butter on rib-eye steak and place it in the refrigerator for 30 minutes
3. Place marinated steak on air fryer oven pan and cook at 400 F for 12-14 minutes. Serve and enjoy.

Nutrition: Calories 416 Fat 36.7 g Carbs 0.7 g Protein 20.3 g

25.   Classic Beef Jerky

Preparation Time: 10 minutes

Cooking Time: 4 hours

Servings: 4

Ingredients:

- 2 lbs. London broil, sliced thinly
- 1 tsp onion powder
- 3 tbsp. brown sugar
- 3 tbsp. soy sauce
- 1 tsp olive oil
- 3/4 tsp garlic powder

Directions:

1. Add all ingredients except meat in the large zip-lock bag.
2. Mix until well combined. Add meat in the bag.
3. Seal bag and massage gently to cover the meat with marinade.
4. Let marinate the meat for 1 hour.
5. Arrange marinated meat slices on air fryer tray and dehydrate at 160 F for 4 hours.

Nutrition: Calories 133 Fat 4.7 g Carbs 9.4 g Protein 13.4 g

Fish & Seafood

26.   Crab Cakes

Preparation Time: 25 minutes

Cooking Time: 15 minutes

Servings: 3

Ingredients:

- 1 egg
- 2tbsps. Mayonnaise
- 1 tsp. Old Bay Seasoning.
- 1/2 tsp. salt
- 2 tbsps. Fresh parsley (diced)
- 1 cup fresh crab meat
- 1 cup saltines (crushed)
- 1/2 cup panko
- 1 onion (peeled and diced)
- 1/2 tsp. Dijon mustard
- 1 tsp. Worcestershire sauce

Directions:

1. Mix together mayonnaise, onion, Dijon mustard, egg, old Bay seasoning, Worcestershire, saltines, salt and parsley in a bowl
2. Pour the crab in the mixture and mix properly.
3. Make the crab mixture into patties, then soak them into the panko allowing the both side to coat well
4. Put it in the fridge for about 1 hour

5. Spray the crab cake on both sides with oil

6. Set into the air fryer and cook at 350 F for 15 minutes. Enjoy!

Nutrition: Calories: 298 kcal Protein: 19.44 g Fat: 8.25 g Carbohydrates: 37.76 g

27. Lobster Tails

Preparation Time: 10 minutes

Cooking Time: 7 minutes

Servings: 3

Ingredients:

- 4 lobster tails (thawed)
- 1 tsp. of pepper
- 2 tbsp. of melted butter
- 1/2 tsp. of salt

Directions:

1. Melt the butter
2. With kitchen scissors, cut lobster right through the tail part

3. Then break the shell and pull backwards with your fingers

4. Rub the lobster tail with butter and add salt and pepper

5. Place it in the air fryer and cook at 380f for 4 minutes

6. Add melted butter and cook for another 3 minutes

7. Serve with more butter

Nutrition: Calories: 255 kcal Protein: 35.55 g Fat: 11.23 g Carbohydrates: 1.42 g

28.   Breaded Shrimp

Preparation Time: 15 minutes

Cooking Time: 11 minutes

Servings: 3

Ingredients:

- 1-pound of shrimp, peeled and deveined
- 2 eggs
- 1/2 cup of panko
- 1/2 cup of onion, peeled and diced
- 1 tsp. of ginger
- 1 tsp. of garlic powder
- 1 tsp. of black pepper

Directions:

1. Preheat air fryer to 350 F
2. Crack the eggs in a bowl
3. Then combine onion, panko and spices in another bowl
4. Sink the shrimps in the eggs and then in the panko bowl
5. Air fry for about 6 minutes, turn over the shrimps and cook for another 5 minutes
6. Serve and enjoy

Nutrition: Calories:279 kcal Protein: 39.48 g Fat: 10.57 g Carbohydrates: 3.96 g

29. Salmon with Mustard Sauce

Preparation Time: 10 minutes

Cooking Time: 8 minutes

Servings: 2-4

Ingredients:

- 1/4 cup honey
- 1/4 cup Dijon mustard
- 2–4 pieces salmon
- 1/2 cup mayonnaise

Directions:

1. Make a salmon fillet
2. Cut the salmon into desired pieces
3. Then combine together mayo, honey, Dijon mustard, salt, and pepper in a bowl then leave the rest for dipping sauce
4. Spread the mixture on the salmon fillets
5. Spray the air fryer basket and put the salmon in it
6. Cook at 400f for about 8 minutes
7. Remove from air fryer and serve with remaining side sauce

Nutrition: Calories:191 kcal Protein: 4.03 g Fat: 11.57 g Carbohydrates: 19.29 g

30.   Sweet And Sour Shrimp

Preparation Time: 5 minutes

Cooking Time: 5 minutes

Servings: 3

Ingredients:

- 1-pound shrimp, peeled and deveined

- 1/2 cup sweet and sour sauce

Directions:

1. Combine the shrimps, sweet and sour sauce together in a bowl

2. Then spread on the air fryer tray and put it in air fryer

3. Cook at 400f for 5 minutes and serve

Nutrition: Calories: 226 kcal Protein: 32.65 g Fat: 2.8 g Carbohydrates: 17.84 g

31.   Fish Cakes

Preparation Time: 15 minutes

Cooking Time: 12 minutes

Servings: 3

Ingredients:

- Nonstick cooking spray
- 10 ounces finely chopped white fish
- ⅔ Cup whole-wheat panko breadcrumbs
- 3 tsp. finely chopped fresh cilantro
- 2 tsp. Thai sweet chili sauce
- 2 tsp. canola mayonnaise
- 1 large eggs
- ⅛ Tsp. salt
- ¼ teaspoon ground pepper
- 2 lime wedges

Directions:

1. Oil the air fryer basket with cooking spray
2. Mix together egg, chili sauce, fish, panko, cilantro, mayonnaise, salt and pepper in a bowl
3. Mold the mixture into 3-inch size cake
4. Spray the cake with cooking spray and put it in the air fryer basket
5. Cook at 380f for about 12 minutes or till the cakes are brown and the inner temperature reads 140f

6. Serve with lime wedges and enjoy

Nutrition: Calories: 196 kcal Protein: 21.04 g Fat: 7.07 g Carbohydrates: 12.21 g

32.   Cod

Preparation Time: 15 minutes

Cooking Time: 11 minutes

Servings: 4

Ingredients:

- 1-pound of cod

- 1 egg

- 1/2 tsp. salt

- 1/8 tsp. black pepper

- 1/2 cup all-purpose flour

- 1 1/2 cups panko breadcrumbs or regular breadcrumbs

- 2 tsp. taco seasoning (optional)

- 1 teaspoon Italian seasoning or old bay seasoning

Directions:

1. Preheat your air fryer to 400F

2. Pat the cod dry, place on cutting board set aside

3. Whisk the egg in a bowl.

4. Pour flour in another bowl

5. Then panko breadcrumbs, pepper, salt and taco seasoning in the third bowl and mix well.

6. Dip the cod into the egg and wet the 2 sides, and transfer to the bowl of flour and press into the flour on both sides.

7. Then Move the cod to the panko breadcrumbs and press both sides into the breadcrumbs.

8. Spray the air fryer with non-stick spray. Add the cod in batches to the air fryer and cook at 400°f for 11 minutes, gently turn around halfway through.

Nutrition: Calories: 264 kcal Protein: 30.37 g Fat: 9 g Carbohydrates: 14.93 g

Preparation Time: 15 minutes

Cooking Time: 7 minutes

Servings: 2

Ingredients:

- Tilapia fillets
- Light spritz of canola oil from an oil spritz
- Old bay seasoning

- Lemon pepper

- Salt

- Molly Mcbutter or butter buds

Directions:

1. Defrost fillets, if frozen then Spray air fryer basket with cooking spray.

2. Place fillets in the basket and season to taste with the spices. Spray little oil.

3. Set air fryer to 400f for 7 minutes. Check for doneness after the timer goes off, Fish should flake easily with a fork.

4. Serve and enjoy with your favorite veggies.

Nutrition: Calories: 106 kcal Protein: 15.3 g Fat: 4.06 g Carbohydrates: 2.13 g

Vegetable, Soup & Stew

Preparation Time: 5 minutes

Cooking Time: 15 minutes

Servings: 8

Ingredients:

- 1-pound Brussels sprouts, trimmed

- 2 cups kale, torn

- 1 tablespoon olive oil

- Salt and black pepper to the taste

- 3 ounces mozzarella, shredded

Directions:

1. In a pan that fits the air fryer, combine all the ingredients except the mozzarella and toss.

2. Put the pan in the air fryer and cook at 380 degrees F for 15 minutes.

3. Divide between plates, sprinkle the cheese on top and serve.

Nutrition: Calories 170 Fat 5 Fiber 3 Carbs 4 Protein 7

35.   Spicy Olives and Avocado Mix

Preparation Time: 5 minutes

Cooking Time: 15 minutes

Servings: 4

Ingredients:

- 2 cups kalamata olives, pitted
- 2 small avocados, pitted, peeled and sliced
- ¼ cup cherry tomatoes, halved
- Juice of 1 lime
- 1 tablespoon coconut oil, melted

Directions:

1. In a pan that fits the air fryer, combine the olives with the other ingredients, toss, put the pan in your air fryer and cook at 370 degrees F for 15 minutes.

2. Divide the mix between plates and serve.

Nutrition: Calories 153 Fat 3 Fiber 3 Carbs 4 Protein 6

36. Olives, Green beans and Bacon

Preparation Time: 5 minutes

Cooking Time: 15 minutes

Servings: 4

Ingredients:

- ½ pound green beans, trimmed and halved
- 1 cup black olives, pitted and halved
- ¼ cup bacon, cooked and crumbled
- 1 tablespoon olive oil
- ¼ cup tomato sauce

Directions:

1. In a pan that fits the air fryer, combine all the ingredients, toss, put the pan in the air fryer and cook at 380 degrees F for 15 minutes.

2. Divide between plates and serve.

Nutrition: Calories 160 Fat 4 Fiber 3 Carbs 5 Protein 4

37.   Cajun Olives and Peppers

Preparation Time: 4 minutes

Cooking Time: 12 minutes

Servings: 4

Ingredients:

- 1 tablespoon olive oil
- ½ pound mixed bell peppers, sliced
- 1 cup black olives, pitted and halved
- ½ tablespoon Cajun seasoning

Directions:

1. In a pan that fits the air fryer, combine all the ingredients.
2. Put the pan it in your air fryer and cook at 390 degrees F for 12 minutes.
3. Divide the mix between plates and serve.

Nutrition: Calories 151 Fat 3 Fiber 2 Carbs 4 Protein 5

38.   Crisp Kale

Preparation Time: 5 Minutes

Cooking Time: 8 Minutes

Servings: 4

Ingredients:

- 4 Handfuls Kale, Washed & Stemless

- 1 Tablespoon Olive Oil

- Pinch Sea Salt

Directions:

1. Start by heating it to 360, and then combine your ingredients together making sure your kale is coated evenly.

2. Place the kale in your fryer and cook for eight minutes.

Nutrition: Calories: 121 Fat: 4 Carbs: 5 Protein: 8

39.   Simple Basil Potatoes

Preparation Time: 15 Minutes

Cooking Time: 40 Minutes

Servings: 4

Ingredients:

- 18 Medium Potatoes
- 5 Tablespoons Olive Oil
- 4 Teaspoons Basil, Dried
- 1 ½ Teaspoons Garlic Powder
- Salt & Pepper to Taste
- Ounces Butter

Directions:

1. Turn on your air fryer to 390.

2. Cut your potatoes lengthwise, and make sure to cut them thin.

3. Lightly coat your potatoes with both your butter and oil.

4. Add in salt and pepper, and then cook for 40 minutes.

Nutrition: Calories: 140 Fat: 5 Carbs: 8 Protein: 9

40.   Air fryer Mediterranean Lentil and Collard Soup

Preparation Time: 10 minutes

Cooking Time: 20 minutes

Servings: 6

Ingredients:

- 2 tablespoons of extra virgin olive oil
- 1 medium yellow onion, chopped
- 2 medium celery stocks, diced
- 3 garlic cloves, minced
- 2 teaspoons of ground cumin
- 1 teaspoon of ground turmeric
- 4 cups of low-sodium vegetable broth
- 1 ¼ cup of water
- 1 1/2 cups brown lentils, rinsed in water
- 2 carrots, peeled and diced
- 1 bay leaf
- 1 teaspoon himalayan salt
- ½ teaspoon of ground black pepper
- 3 collard leaves, cut into strips
- 1 teaspoon of lemon juice

Directions:

1. Set air fryer to saute, then add the olive oil, heat, and add onions and celery. Stir often for 5 minutes. Turn the air fryer off.

2. Stir in the garlic, cumin, and turmeric until combined.

3. Add broth, water, lentils, carrots, bay leaf, salt, and pepper. Lock the lid and close the valve. Fix to manual and cook on high pressure for 13 minutes.

4. After completion, quick release the pressure, carefully remove the lid and stir in collards and lemon juice.

5. Make sure to lock the lid and set to manual and cook for 2 more minutes on high. Quick-release the pressure, open the lid, and it's ready to serve.

Nutrition: Calories – 127.9 Protein – 7.3 g. Fat – 0.8 g. Carbs – 25.9 g.

41. Green Chicken Chili

Preparation Time: 10 minutes

Cooking Time: 35 minutes

Servings: 8

Ingredients:

- 2 tbsp. unsalted butter
- 1 medium yellow onion (to be peeled and chopped)
- ½ lb. poblano peppers (to be seeded and roughly chopped)
- ½ lb. Anaheim peppers (to be seeded and roughly chopped)
- ½ lb. tomatillos (to be husked and quartered)
- 2 small jalapeño peppers (to be seeded and roughly chopped)
- 2 garlic cloves (to be peeled and minced)

- 1 tsp. ground cumin

- 6 bone-in, skin-on chicken thighs (2 ½ lbs. in total)

- 2 cups chicken stock

- 2 cups water

- 1/3 cup roughly chopped fresh cilantro

- 3 cans Great Northern beans (to be drained and rinsed, 15 oz. cans)

Directions:

1. Choose the "Sauté" button on the Air fryer and when hot, add butter to melt.

2. Once the butter melts, add onion and cook for about 3 minutes until softened. Add poblano and Anaheim peppers, then tomatillos, and jalapeños. Cook 3 minutes add garlic and cumin. Cook about 30 seconds or until fragrant. Then cancel sautéing.

3. Add the thighs, stock, and water to pot and stir.

4. Tightly close lid and have the steam release set to the "Sealing" position. Select the "Rice/Grain" option and set the timer for 30 minutes.

5. At the end of the cook time, do a quick release of pressure and open lid to stir well. Press the "Cancel" button and transfer the chicken to a cutting board. After carefully removing the skin, shred the meat with two forks.

6. Using an immersion blender, purée the sauce until smooth.

7. Stir in the meat, cilantro, and beans and serve warm.

Nutrition: Calories – 304 Protein – 33 g. Fat – 10 g. Carbs – 19 g.

42. Air fryer Italian Beef Stew

Preparation Time: 10 minutes

Cooking Time: 35 minutes

Servings: 6

Ingredients:

- 3 pounds of beef stew
- 1 onion, diced
- 4 carrots, diced
- 8-ounce baby portabella mushrooms, sliced
- 24-ounces of beef broth
- 15 ounce diced tomatoes, canned
- 3 tablespoons of white flour
- 1 teaspoon of dried basil leaves
- 1 teaspoon of dried thyme leaves
- 1 teaspoon of salt
- 1 teaspoon of pepper
- dried parsley

Directions:

1. Place meat in the air fryer.
2. Add in carrots, broth, flour, basil, thyme, salt, pepper, and tomatoes to air fryer and stir.
3. Close the lid.
4. Cook on high pressure for 35 minutes.

5. Quick release the pressure and carefully remove the lid.

6. Stir in the mushroom, stir the soup and then serve.

Nutrition: Calories – 385 Protein – 54 g. Fat – 12 g. Carbs – 12 g.

Snack & Dessert

43. Steamed Pot Stickers

Preparation Time: 20 minutes

Cooking Time: 10 minutes

Servings: 10

Ingredients:

- ½ cup finely chopped cabbage
- ¼ cup finely chopped red bell pepper
- 2 green onions, finely chopped
- 1 egg, beaten
- 2 tablespoons cocktail sauce
- 2 teaspoons low-sodium soy sauce
- 30 wonton wrappers
- 3 tablespoons water, plus more for brushing the wrappers

Directions:

1. In a small bowl, combine the cabbage, pepper, green onions, egg, cocktail sauce, and soy sauce, and mix well.

2. Put about 1 teaspoon of the mixture in the center of each wonton wrapper. Fold the wrapper in half, covering the filling dampen the edges with water, and seal. You can crimp the edges of the wrapper with your fingers so they look like the pot stickers you get in restaurants. Brush them with water.

3. Put 3 tablespoons water in the pan under the air fryer basket. Cook the pot stickers in 2 batches for 9 to 10 minutes or until the pot stickers are hot and the bottoms are lightly browned.

4. Substitution tip: Use other vegetables in this recipe, such as corn, baby peas, or chopped zucchini or summer squash. You could also add leftover cooked meat such as pork or chicken, finely chopped.

Nutrition: Calories 291; Fat 2g Carbs 57g Protein 10g

44.   Beef and Mango Skewers

Preparation Time: 10 minutes

Cooking Time: 5 minutes

Servings: 4

Ingredients:

- ¾ pound beef sirloin tip, cut into 1-inch cubes
- 2 tablespoons balsamic vinegar
- 1 tablespoon olive oil
- 1 tablespoon honey
- ½ teaspoon dried marjoram
- Pinch salt
- Freshly ground black pepper
- 1 mango

Directions:

1. Put the beef cubes in a medium bowl and add the balsamic vinegar, olive oil, honey, marjoram, salt, and pepper. Mix well, and then massage the marinade into the beef with your hands. Set aside.

2. To prepare the mango, stand it on end and cut the skin off, using a sharp knife. Then carefully cut around the oval pit to remove the flesh. Cut the mango into 1-inch cubes.

3. Thread metal skewers alternating with three beef cubes and two mango cubes.

4. Grill the skewers in the air fryer basket for 4 to 7 minutes or until the beef is browned and at least 145°F.

Nutrition: Calories 242; Fat 9g Carbs 13g Protein 26g

Preparation Time: 5 minutes

Cooking Time: 12 minutes

Servings: 4

Ingredients:

- ½ cup sour cream
- ½ cup mango chutney
- 3 teaspoons curry powder, divided
- 4 cups frozen sweet potato fries
- 1 tablespoon olive oil
- Pinch salt
- Freshly ground black pepper

Directions:

1. In a small bowl, combine sour cream, chutney, and 1½ teaspoons of the curry powder. Mix well and set aside. Put the sweet potatoes in a medium bowl. Drizzle with the olive oil and sprinkle with remaining 1½ teaspoons curry powder, salt, and pepper.

2. Put the potatoes in the air fryer basket. Cook for 8 to 12 minutes or until crisp, hot, and golden brown, shaking the basket once during cooking time. Place the fries in a serving basket and serve with the chutney dip.

3. Substitution tip: You can use fresh sweet potatoes in place of the frozen precut fries. Use one or two sweet potatoes, peel them, and cut into ⅓-inch thick strips using a sharp knife or mandoline. Use as directed in recipe; but you will need to increase the cooking time.

Nutrition: Calories 323; Fat 10g Carbs 58g Protein 3g

46. Spicy Kale Chips with Yogurt Sauce

Preparation Time: 10 minutes

Cooking Time: 5 minutes

Servings: 4

Ingredients:

- 1 cup Greek yogurt
- 3 tablespoons lemon juice
- 2 tablespoons honey mustard
- ½ teaspoon dried oregano
- 1 bunch curly kale
- 2 tablespoons olive oil
- ½ teaspoon salt
- ⅛ Teaspoon pepper

Directions:

1. In a small bowl, combine the yogurt, lemon juice, honey mustard, and oregano, and set aside.

2. Remove the stems and ribs from the kale with a sharp knife. Cut the leaves into 2- to 3-inch pieces.

3. Toss the kale with olive oil, salt, and pepper. Massage the oil into the leaves with your hands.

4. Air-fry the kale in batches until crisp, about 5 minutes, shaking the basket once during cooking time. Serve with the yogurt sauce.

5. Ingredient tip: Kale comes in several different varieties. Tuscan (also known as dinosaur or lacinato) kale is the sturdiest and makes excellent chips. Curly kale, the variety most widely found in grocery stores, can become slightly frizzy when cooked in the air fryer, but is still delicious.

Nutrition: Calories 154; Fat 8g Carbs 13g Protein 8g

47. Phyllo Artichoke Triangles

Preparation Time: 15 minutes

Cooking Time: 10 minutes

Servings: 14

Ingredients:

- ¼ cup ricotta cheese

- 1 egg white

- ⅓Cup minced Dry-out artichoke hearts

- 3 tablespoons grated mozzarella cheese

- ½ teaspoon dried thyme

- 6 sheets frozen phyllo dough, thawed

- 2 tablespoons melted butter

Directions:

1. In a small bowl, combine ricotta cheese, egg white, artichoke hearts, mozzarella cheese, and thyme, and mix well. Cover the phyllo dough with a damp kitchen towel while you work so it doesn't dry out. Place on the work surface and cut into thirds lengthwise using one sheet at a time.

2. Put about 1½ teaspoons of the filling on each strip at the base. Fold the bottom right-hand tip of phyllo over the filling to meet the other side in a triangle, and then continue folding in a triangle. Brush each triangle with butter to seal the edges. Repeat with remaining phyllo dough and filling.

3. Bake, 6 at a time, for about 3 to 4 minutes or until the phyllo is golden brown and crisp.

4. Substitution tip: You can use anything in this filling in place of the artichoke hearts. Try spinach, chopped cooked shrimp, cooked sausage, or keep it vegetarian and use all grated cheese.

Nutrition: Calories 271 Fat 17g Carbs 23g Protein 9g

48.   Spinach Dip with Bread Knots

Preparation Time: 12 minutes

Cooking Time: 20 minutes

Servings: 6

Ingredients:

- Nonstick cooking spray

- 1 (8-ounce) package cream cheese, cut into cubes

- ¼ cup sour cream

- ½ cup frozen chopped spinach, thawed and Dry-out

- ½ cup grated Swiss cheese

- 2 green onions, chopped

- ½ (11-ounce) can refrigerated breadstick dough

- 2 tablespoons melted butter

- 3 tablespoons grated Parmesan cheese

Directions:

1. Spray a 6-by-6-by-2-inch pan with nonstick cooking spray.

2. In a medium bowl, combine the cream cheese, sour cream, spinach, Swiss cheese, and green onions, and mix well. Spread into the prepared pan and Bake it for 8 minutes or until hot. While the dip is baking, unroll six of the breadsticks and cut them in half crosswise to make 12 pieces.

3. Gently stretch each piece of dough and tie into a loose knot; tuck in the ends.

4. When the dip is hot, remove from the air fryer and carefully place each bread knot on top of the dip, covering the surface of the dip. Brush each knot with melted butter and sprinkle Parmesan cheese on top.

5. Bake it for 8 to 13 minutes or until the bread knots are golden brown and cooked through.

Nutrition: Calories 264 Fat 23g Carbs 7g Protein 8g

49.   Peanut Butter Cookies

Preparation Time: 2 minutes

Cooking Time: 5 minutes

Servings: 10

Ingredients:

- Peanut Butter: 1 cup

- Sugar: 1 cup

- 1 Egg

Directions:

1. Blend all of the ingredients with a hand mixer.

2. Spray trays of air fryer with canola oil. (Alternatively, parchment paper can also be used, but it will take longer to cook your cookies)

3. Set the air fryer temperature to 350 degrees and preheat it.

4. Place rounded dough balls onto air fryer trays. Press down softly with the back of a fork.

5. Place air fryer tray in your air fryer in the middle place. Cook for five minutes.

6. Use milk to serve with cookies.

Nutrition: Calories – 236 Protein – 6 g. Fat – 13 g. Carbs – 26 g.

Preparation Time: 10 minutes

Cooking Time: 15 minutes

Servings: 4

Ingredients:

- 4 pears, cored and cut into wedges

- 1 tsp vanilla

- 1/4 cup apple juice

- 2 cups grapes, halved

Directions:

1. Put all of the ingredients in the inner pot of air fryer and stir well.

2. Seal pot and cook on high for 15 minutes.

3. As soon as the cooking is done, let it release pressure naturally for 10 minutes then release remaining using quick release. Remove lid.

4. Stir and serve.

Nutrition: Calories – 162 Protein – 1.1 g. Fat – 0.5 g. Carbs – 41.6 g.

Measurement Conversion Chart

CONVERSION CHART

Liquid Measure		Dry Measure		Linear Measure	
8 ounces =	1 cup	2 pints =	1 quart	12 inches =	1 foot
2 cups =	1 pint	4 quarts =	1 gallon	3 feet =	1 yard
16 ounces =	1 pint	8 quarts =	2 gallons or 1 peck	5.5 yards =	1 rod
4 cups =	1 quart			40 rods =	1 furlong
1 gill =	1/2 cup or 1/4 pint	4 pecks =	8 gallons or 1 bushel	8 furlongs (5280 feet) =	1 mile
2 pints =	1 quart	16 ounces =	1 pound	6080 feet =	1 nautical mile
4 quarts =	1 gallon	2000 lbs. =	1 ton		
31.5 gal. =	1 barrel				

3 tsp =	1 tbsp				
2 tbsp =	1/8 cup or 1 fluid ounce				
4 tbsp =	1/4 cup				
8 tbsp =	1/2 cup				
1 pinch =	1/8 tsp or less				
1 tsp =	60 drops				

Conversion of US Weight and Mass Measure to Metric System

.0353 ounces =	1 gram
1/4 ounce =	7 grams
1 ounce =	28.35 grams
4 ounces =	113.4 grams
8 ounces =	226.8 grams
1 pound =	454 grams
2.2046 pounds =	1 kilogram
.98421 long ton or 1.1023 short tons =	1 metric ton

Conversion of US Liquid Measure to Metric System

1 fluid oz. =	29.573 milliliters
1 cup =	230 milliliters
1 quart =	.94635 liters
1 gallon =	3.7854 liters
.033814 fluid ounce =	1 milliliter
3.3814 fluid ounces =	1 deciliter
33.814 fluid oz. or 1.0567 qt. =	1 liter

Conversion of US Linear Measure to Metric System

1 inch =	2.54 centimeters
1 foot =	.3048 meters
1 yard =	.9144 meters
1 mile =	1609.3 meters or 1.6093 kilometers
.03937 in. =	1 millimeter
.3937 in. =	1 centimeter
3.937 in. =	1 decimeter
39.37 in. =	1 meter
3280.8 ft. or .62137 miles =	1 kilometer

To convert a Fahrenheit temperature to Centigrade, do the following:
a. Subtract 32   b. Multiply by 5   c. Divide by 9

To convert Centigrade to Fahrenheit, do the following:
a. Multiply by 9   b. Divide by 5   c. Add 32

AIR FRYER COOKING TIMES

	Temperature (°F)	Time (min)		Temperature (°F)	Time (min)
Vegetables					
Asparagus (sliced 1-inch)	400°F	5	Onions (pearl)	400°F	10
Beets (whole)	400°F	40	Parsnips (½-inch chunks)	380°F	15
Broccoli (florets)	400°F	6	Peppers (1-inch chunks)	400°F	15
Brussels Sprouts (halved)	380°F	15	Potatoes (small baby, 1.5 lbs)	400°F	15
Carrots (sliced ½-inch)	380°F	15	Potatoes (1-inch chunks)	400°F	12
Cauliflower (florets)	400°F	12	Potatoes (baked whole)	400°F	40
Corn on the cob	390°F	6	Squash (½-inch chunks)	400°F	12
Eggplant (1½-inch cubes)	400°F	15	Sweet Potato (baked)	380°F	30 to 35
Fennel (quartered)	370°F	15	Tomatoes (cherry)	400°F	4
Green Beans	400°F	5	Tomatoes (halves)	350°F	10
Kale leaves	250°F	12	Zucchini (½-inch sticks)	400°F	12
Mushrooms (sliced ¼-inch)	400°F	5			
Chicken					
Breasts, bone in (1.25 lbs.)	370°F	25	Legs, bone in (1.75 lbs.)	380°F	30
Breasts, boneless (4 oz.)	380°F	12	Wings (2 lbs.)	400°F	12
Drumsticks (2.5 lbs.)	370°F	20	Game Hen (halved - 2 lbs.)	390°F	20
Thighs, bone in (2 lbs.)	380°F	22	Whole Chicken (6.5 lbs.)	360°F	75
Thighs, boneless (1.5 lbs.)	380°F	18 to 20	Tenders	360°F	8 to 10
Beef					
Burger (4 oz.)	370°F	16 to 20	Meatballs (3-inch)	380°F	10
Filet Mignon (8 oz.)	400°F	18	Ribeye, bone in (1-inch, 8 oz.)	400°F	10 to15
Flank Steak (1.5 lbs.)	400°F	12	Sirloin steaks (1-inch, 12 oz.)	400°F	9 to 14
London Broil (2 lbs.)	400°F	20 to 28	Beef Eye Round Roast (4 lbs.)	390°F	45 to 55
Meatballs (1-inch)	380°F	7			
Pork and Lamb					
Loin (2 lbs.)	360°F	55	Bacon (thick cut)	400°F	6 to 10
Pork Chops, bone in (1-inch, 6.5 oz.)	400°F	12	Sausages	380°F	15
Tenderloin (1 lb.)	370°F	15	Lamb Loin Chops (1-inch thick)	400°F	8 to 12
Bacon (regular)	400°F	5 to 7	Rack of lamb (1.5 - 2 lbs.)	380°F	22
Fish and Seafood					
Calamari (8 oz.)	400°F	4	Tuna steak	400°F	7 to 10
Fish Fillet (1-inch, 8 oz.)	400°F	10	Scallops	400°F	5 to 7
Salmon, fillet (6 oz.)	380°F	12	Shrimp	400°F	5
Swordfish steak	400°F	10			